YARD

VINEYARD

A YEAR IN THE LIFE OF CALIFORNIA'S WINE COUNTRY

JOY STERLING

PHOTOGRAPHY BY ANDY KATZ

SIMON & SCHUSTER EDITIONS

JOY

—

To the future

ANDY

—

To Kathy & Jesse

SIMON & SCHUSTER EDITIONS
Rockefeller Center
1230 Avenue of the Americas
New York, New York 10020
Simon & Schuster Editions and colophon are trademarks
of Simon & Schuster Inc.

Designed by Joel Avirom and Jason Snyder
Design Assistant: Meghan Day Healey

Manufactured in Italy

10 9 8 7 6 5 4 3 2 1

Library of Congress Cataloging-in-Publication Data
Sterling, Joy.
    Vineyard : a year in the life of California's wine country / Joy Sterling
and Andy Katz.
        p.   cm.
        1. Wine and wine making—California—Pictorial works. I. Katz,
    Andy, date. II. Title.
    TP557.S733   1998
    641.2'2'09794—dc21   98-18194
                                                          CIP

ISBN 0-684-83930-X

*I happily and lovingly acknowledge my husband,
Forrest Tancer, and my parents, Audrey and Barry Sterling,
who help me in everything I do; Dan Green, J. B. Meaders,
and Janice Easton. Thank you.*

JOY STERLING

*I would like to thank Forrest and Joy for their love and
support and for making this book happen. To the passionate,
talented people involved in the wine business whom I have
been fortunate enough to become friends with, as well as
Dan Green, Janice Easton, Joel Avirom, Robert and
Susan Katz, and Michael Ditch.*

ANDY KATZ

CONTENTS

California Wine Country 12

The Passion with Perspective 18

The Prayers for Balanced Weather 24

The Sculpting of the Vines 32

The Abundance of the Blooms 42

The Philosophy of Growth 50

Hope Through Adversity 54

The Investment for the Future 66

The Search for Favorable Omens 72

The Beginning of Harvest 80

The Alchemy of the Blend 88

The Preparation for Rest 92

A NOTE FROM THE PHOTOGRAPHER 96

VINEYARD

There's no doubt that we're spoiled in California. Our lives revolve around fresh flowers and Eden-like fruits and vegetables. We're accustomed to having our own olive oil, herbs at our doorstep, farm-fresh cheeses, baby lamb and quail directly from the farmers, Dungeness crab and wild salmon right out of the water.

Just an innocent stroll through our local grocery store can incur intense envy from visitors because of the ten varieties of mushrooms, blood oranges every day, and an array of shiny black and green home-cured olives: plain, garlicky, marinated with coriander, and stuffed with sun-dried tomatoes or Habanero peppers, which even after a warning to be careful can be killingly hot. With this sheer abundance and diversity, there's an intrinsic brightness of flavor to everything we grow here.

We have a strong, long-lived wine culture, dating back to the Spanish missions, when in the 1760s wine was first made to supply the sacrament for mass. The first commercial winery was bonded in 1839 in Cucamonga, near Los Angeles, then a dusty pueblo. Initially the California wine trade was concentrated in the Southland, and it seems to be headed back down that way with the emergence of Santa Barbara Chardonnays and Pinot Noirs in the past ten years and, even more recently, San Diego Syrahs.

New areas are still being developed. An example is Petaluma in southern Sonoma County, where hundreds of acres are being planted. This used to be cattle grazing country, and Petaluma once billed itself as the chicken capital of the world. You can still see a few collapsed, old, redwood chicken coops along the Old Gravenstein Highway, but they're disintegrating into the ground the way a felled tree eventually fades away in the undergrowth.

Twenty years ago my husband, Forrest, predicted it was an upcoming area because of the incursions of fog through the Petaluma Gap, a small notch in the coastal range, from which Russian River and Green Valley get the spillover. The problem was that there just wasn't any water to do the planting. Now, though, just about any engineering problem can be solved with enough money, and Petaluma may well be borne out as one of the greatest grape-growing regions in the world.

I think few people realize that in the 1890s California wine—primarily from Napa and Sonoma—was as highly regarded internationally as it is today. The draw north was largely because of the Gold Rush, which suddenly generated a population in Northern California—proof that it takes a good market to make good wine. We were the up-and-coming wine-producing area of the world, and the winemakers then, as now, were dreamers, hopeless romantics and great promoters, as big and flamboyant as hot-air balloons. One of the most famous wineries of the time was La Questa—known especially for Cabernet Sauvignon—which naturally wowed the rest of the wine-drinking world with its gorgeous, vibrant, exuberant California fruit.

Robert Louis Stevenson wrote about the vineyards being planted along the Silverado trail. He compared it to prospecting—first you try one varietal in a certain soil, then another, and another, until you hit pay dirt. But, who knows? Experimentation may be an inherent quality of California wine—that the quest for newness is part of what makes it American—while in France there is

an ongoing fight, both in food and wine, whether to respect the canon or be innovative.

In some ways, the competition a hundred years ago was less fierce than it is today. European winemaking of the era was so "backward"—folklore compared to modern techniques—that a bad vintage was an unavoidable disaster. California ruled on climate alone.

We went into a kind of dark age beginning in 1920— forty years of Prohibition, the Depression, World War II; then, in the 1950s, there was a propensity to ship undistinguished French Colombard, Chenin Blanc, or Carignane, indiscrimi‚ nately marketed as Chablis or Burgundy. All the while, wine remained very much a part of the California experience. The older generation of San Franciscans still vividly remember the yeasty smell of homemade wine fermenting in the basements of North Beach in the 1930s. It sounds vulgar now, but every‚

one then naively and carelessly called it "Dago red," and it was good wine. Louis Martini Jr. emerged from Prohibition as the finest winemaker in the state. The first vintage of Beaulieu Vineyards' Georges De Latour Private Reserve was put into wood barrels in 1936. André Tchelistcheff started making that wine in 1938.

Napa's 1951 vintage was legendary, with masters like Tchelistcheff producing great wine for a very limited but discrimi‚ nating public. Every account of Allen Ginsberg's first reading of *Howl* includes a description of Jack Kerouac beating out the cadence on a half gallon wine jug, which I presume contained Zinfandel. And in 1952 James D. Zellerbach, financier and American Ambassador to Italy, founded Hanzell Winery in Sonoma, which still has a devoted cult following for Chardonnay.

The current golden age began in the late 1960s and early 1970s, coinciding with a revolution in wine that was taking place all over the world. The California winemakers were greatly inspired by what was happening with California food—the quest for freshness, seasonality, baby vegetables, good bread, fresh chèvre, and creative, eclectic cuisine by the likes of Alice Waters and Wolfgang Puck. Some of the big names of this generation are Robert Mondavi (below), who set the standard for innovative winemaking techniques and being open to experimentation; Chuck Wagner, who founded Caymus in 1972; Warren Winiarski of Stags Leap; Joseph Phelps, who pioneered the concept of Bordeaux-style blending in California; and Joe Heitz, who remains obstinate about single-vineyard Cabernet.

Today, delicious wine comes from everywhere, making all of us acutely aware that we're only as good as our last vintage. And while we may strive always to be cutting edge, we certainly don't want to be cut off from the past. The tradition is such that a winemaker like John Williams of Frog's Leap takes making Napa Valley Cabernet as an "awesome responsibility—the ultimate achievement of our craft" and half-jokingly says he will have to prove himself with a vertical of his Cabs to qualify for heaven.

Of course, living in the vineyards and making Cabernet may already be heaven.

Food and wine continue to grow and evolve together, each urging and encouraging the other to raise the ante. We tend to think of the vineyards as an extension of the gardens—or vice versa—all part of the same bounty. The geographic spread, the diversity of landscapes, innumerable combinations of soil, slope, elevation, the dramatic encounter of mountain and ocean, the ebb and flow of the fog, all make California a winemaker's paradise of possibilities.

For a long time, I think it was a major psychological hurdle that having better weather than Bordeaux or Burgundy was actually somehow a disadvantage—that wine, like a suffering artist, required marginal circumstances to achieve greatness. But we've now wrestled that issue to the ground, as has everyone else. I can virtually guarantee that every year is a vintage year somewhere in the world.

Despite the relative ease of cultivation, no two years are alike in California wine country. Each vintage has distinctions—two equally fine years can still taste very different—and in our best wines, we try to deliver, in the bottle, a kind of record of everything we saw, smelled, and sensed throughout that particular growing season. In a way, winemakers are like photographers capturing a place and a moment. Both involve passion and perspective, and if a photograph is worth a thousand words, how many might a sip of wine be worth? Our focus is the vineyard. Each has a story, its own romantic tale of how it came to be whether because of a landfall from a mountain ten thousand years ago or the changed path of a river. You could still find Wappo Indian arrowheads in the vineyards around Calistoga as recently as the 1970s.

A vintage rarely favors every grape equally. Even sister varieties like Cabernet Sauvignon and Merlot, and different soils in the same microclimate, like Pomerol and St. Emilion, can yield disparate results because one has naturally better drainage than the other.

Our lives are unusual for being so tied to the land. We wake up and go to sleep with the grapes. In late winter we tend to become sluggish and slip into a kind of hibernation as the vines go dormant. In the spring the frost alarm is hooked up right next to the bed. The more we love a vineyard, the more we grow in sync with it.

Each vintage is completely entwined with our personal lives. We value the emotional quality of certain vintages as much as the quality of the grapes. Birth years and anniversary wines are very important. Certainly 1945 is an example of a strongly felt vintage in France. I believe 1999 will be an emotionally charged vintage—at least for winemakers—all over the world.

So much depends on the weather. Weather makes the vintage. And like farmers everywhere, we're never satisfied. During a gorgeous spring we'll ask for rain, but just a little and preferably at night. We get sore necks from looking up at the sky all of the time.

What are the criteria of a great vintage? In Napa, the most memorable also tend to be the coolest. In Burgundy, the best are the years when picking starts late. A made-to-order vintage for the Russian River is cool and foggy in the summer, followed by a dry, warm September and October.

All winemakers hope for a long growing season. The longer the grapes stay on the vine, the more they will accumulate flavor. Besides concentration, the acidity and the tannins also "ripen" with time on the vine to achieve a natural balance that you can taste in the grape and in the juice as it comes out of the press.

Still, certain years can fool you. One that seemed all out of whack at harvest can, as the wines evolve, become a favorite, especially for Pinot Noir. Some things just take time.

The 1996 vintage stands out for being very wet. I lost track of how many times the bridge at the entrance to Iron Horse was flooded in February and March. The whole vegetable garden was a lake. My most poignant memory of that winter was seeing two white Muscovy ducks swimming down our road.

You can't very well work in the vineyards when it's raining—you just sink to your knees—so we prune the vines as weather permits. There's nothing we can do except wait.

We've had three wet years in a row. We're getting very good at flooding and power outages. Our cover crops between the rows of the vines to hold up the soil against erosion are gorgeous, and we've made do by cooking cioppino on a camp stove. But I'm concerned we won't know how to cope with drought when it comes back around.

Our last drought year was 1991, ending seven years in that cycle, and now we strain to remember what it is like to worry about having enough water to frost-protect or irrigate the vegetables. We would consider it a tragedy to have to stop watering the flowers.

As winter progresses, on the days you can get into the vineyard, you can see where the vineyard workers have been by the contrast of a section that's perfectly manicured next to one that looks wild with all the twisted arms and tangled manes that need to be sorted out and pruned.

The bark of the vines, wet from rain, are a dark, chocolate brown, and the sharp rows of cover crop between the vines—primarily orchard grass, fava beans, and clover—are incredibly green, thick, and textured like chenille. It is bone-chillingly cold and wet. The sky is a volatile mixture of clouds and fog. Decidedly duck weather. The willows along the creek bed have turned a rust color, and the oaks are dripping with Spanish moss. It's exceptionally quiet. I can't think of many other places where you can be at one with nature and your work at the same time.

*I*t takes ten men two hours to prune seven hundred vines—the equivalent of one acre, though that can vary with how densely the vines are planted. The work is very much like pruning roses in terms of the time and consideration lavished on each vine, and it takes a strong, sure, practiced hand to make the cuts.

The goal is to pace the pruning perfectly so the entire vineyard will be ready for budbreak. This is a man-made deadline. You could prune vineyards after budbreak, but the buds are so fragile that you would risk knocking them off, and there's more danger of disease.

The pruners hopscotch around the property, pruning all of the warmer sections of the vineyards first so they'll bud first. There's at least a three-degree temperature difference between our house down by the creek and Thomas Road, which is the highest point on our property. You try to time the pruning so that the colder areas come out later, making them less vulnerable to frost.

As any rosarian will tell you, pruning is like sculpting. Each vine has to be looked at individually and a judgment made on where to cut. It's at this juncture that you can see how one vintage is tied to the next, by how the vine grew the previous year, how much wood you have to work with.

How you prune directly affects the size and quality of the crop. You can imagine how each vine has a certain, finite amount of energy, and where you cut—how many canes you leave and how many buds per cane—determines how that vine's energy is going to be directed. The more wood removed, the more vigorous the regrowth; the fewer the number of

buds, the more you gamble on fewer grapes for deeper flavors. And this is just the first of a thousand compounding gut decisions that set the quality of a wine.

Site and soil are God-given gifts. Each individual vineyard is its own quirky confluence of elements that make it uniquely suited for growing wine. Beyond that it's the unstinting care, passion, dedication, diligence, obsession—whatever you want to call it—that bring a vineyard to prominence.

Left to its own devices, a vine reverts to its natural state as a wild growing liana, which cares nothing for the grapes except to produce seeds. Tending a vineyard—pruning, tying the cordons with twine or green Mylar tape onto the trellising wires, weeding, suckering, spraying with copper and sulfur, retying the shoots as they grow, more suckering, spraying again—involves mundane, unremitting tasks that just have to be done. It takes a loving, acquiescing personality to give them everything they need. Bottom line, it comes down to sheer man-hours invested in the grapes.

Spring is a blaze of yellow with mustard in the fields, the acacias in bloom and champagne-colored sunsets—more like a glow than a color. If you time it right, you can see the start of spring five or six times as you head from Santa Barbara, where in February the mountains are touched with purple and gold, exactly the way Maxfield Parrish would have painted them, up to the more remote-feeling Mendocino. It also repeats itself several times from east to west: from Napa, which is one, long, narrow valley, to the gentle rolling hills of Sonoma. Even on the same vineyard, spring keeps coming—first on the warmer, higher ridges and last in the cool, low-lying areas near a creek or reservoir when the fog settles.

We hold our breath during bloom in May. This is when the crop sets, Mother Nature's first offer in a long process of give and take of how much wine we'll be able to make this year. So much can happen from this point forward—many possibilities of losing the crop—with only one thing for certain: there's no way to get any bigger. But, that's farming.

Flowering lasts about two weeks. You have to look under the leaves to see the forming grapes, capped, tiny, white, pinpoint-size flowers. They turn pink, then brown, and then fall to the ground to let the fruit—smaller than baby green

peas—set behind them. Walking through the vineyards, you might dip down into a vale and suddenly catch the intense, sweet, honey smell in the air.

I would risk touching the flowers only when they're already brown and about to drop off. They seem to float into your hands like a sprinkling of snowflakes: practically weightless, yet powerfully affecting.

We instantly start projecting first the crop size and second when harvest will begin. Sadly, after three short crops in a row, even a "normal" yield—the equivalent of three tons to the acre—seems incredibly abundant.

We hope for at least one hundred days from bloom till harvest, which should be absolutely no problem, if we make it through May without heavy rain or wind. California is largely defined by its dry summers, and we are unique for having the potential of a growing season that can stretch to 130 days.

Not that it would be stress-free. Just halfway through bloom we're already getting shatter in the warmer sections—when the grapes split, as if the energy just bursts out of them, even before they've had a chance to develop.

At this stage in the season, we can optimistically feel that some amount of shatter will simply save us from having to thin the grapes later on; but this is how it starts, that first small chipping away at the crop.

The olive trees bloom simultaneously with the vineyards. In abundant years, their flowers practically change the color of the trees from evergreen to creamy white yellow. Meanwhile the summer vegetable gardens are going in throughout Sonoma County. I love the way they look, disked to an almost Zen-like perfection, though I confess to having a particular affection for freshly turned dirt.

The pace of our lives is accelerating daily. The vines are growing an inch a day. By June they look like a sea of deep green, which at Bernardus in Carmel Valley abuts a steep, heavily forested, jutting mountain. The contrasting, dried-out wild grasses on the Napa and Sonoma hills are the exact color of a golden retriever. You can see the full effects of all the different trellising systems.

All growers like their vineyards trained a certain way. But you can go to any number of them in Napa, Sonoma, or the Central Coast and see widely differing theories—some are low to the ground for warmth or raised eight feet high as they do in Switzerland; some have one wire, two wires, twelve wires, or none at all, like old Zinfandel. And each of us winegrowers emphasizes that while everyone else isn't completely idiotic, ours is the right way for our vineyard.

The old vines are our senior citizens. They're short, about three feet high, and gnarled like an old person's hand. They stand alone, no trellising, and they're head pruned so that the shoots come out of the crown. There are scarcely more than a thousand acres over age fifty statewide, with the greatest concentration in Sonoma County and the Sierra Foothills. They're as much the icons of our history as the keystone from the original winery on Pride Mountain, a Victorian farmhouse nestled in the Alexander Valley, or Robert Mondavi.

The yield from old vines is very low, nature's way of preserving a vine's waning energy, which also has the effect of concentrating flavors. Or perhaps age means that the root systems have reached a point where they suck more nutrients out of the soil, which also adds another facet, more depth, additional nuance, extra complexity—though how deep the roots run depends on the soil.

Many winemakers think the viticultural style of the old vineyards may be as important as the age of the vines, so newly planted Zinfandel is being trained the old way. Of course, you could maintain that much of the allure of old-vine Zinfandel is simply romance, surely a vineyard that wasn't pulled out or switched to another varietal after one hundred years must have something special.

50

The year 1996 saw much replanting, mostly because of phylloxera. Phylloxera is a root louse always present in the soil. There is no antidote for it. The vines must be yanked out by the roots, pushed down on the ground flat on their sides, and left lying in the dust, as though they'd been brought to their knees and shot. The vines are then amassed and burned, the land fumigated and covered with a plastic sheet like a shroud. And we start over, with baby vines in milk and juice cartons all across Napa and Sonoma. One can only hope that the new rootstock we're planting will be resistant.

It amazes me how long it can take for this kind of adversity to run its course. I never really understood before why in the nineteenth century the time span from when phylloxera was first detected in Europe to the end of the blight was at least twenty years. It's a painfully slow death, which this time around has claimed 26,000 acres in Napa and Sonoma since 1982, with an estimated 17,000 acres on vulnerable rootstock to go. It doesn't hit a whole vineyard at once but spreads erratically.

In the short term, the economic bottom line for many vineyards has turned from black to red, at least temporarily, and its effect on California winemaking—indeed, the very taste of the wines—is just starting to show.

Generally speaking, the wines from young vines are lighter bodied, less complex, and less ageworthy than the wines from mature vineyards. They might need to be taken out of the barrel earlier because they can't stand up to as much oak, and they may be released onto the market even earlier than we're accustomed to. Yet, long term, the newly planted vineyards will be of much higher quality because we know so much more about viticulture today—the spacing of the vines, trellising, clonal selection, or improving a vine variety to match a particular soil or climate—than we did in the late 1960s and early 1970s, when most of the vineyards in Napa and Sonoma were developed.

We started replanting Iron Horse in 1996, not because of phylloxera but because the original 110 acres were beginning to fade. Vineyards are by nature organic and temporal and slip away like all living things. It takes three years before the first small harvest, but a vine is said to reach its prime at about twenty-five to thirty, after which it takes considerably more effort to sustain a good crop—a fact of aging I understand perfectly. And each generation is responsible for replanting, reinvesting in the vineyard.

We want to do it as slowly as possible to minimize the annual outflow of money, crop loss, and the impact of young vines on the taste of our wines; but Forrest feels strongly that the future is in the vineyards. Clearly we're not doing this for the short term. All of our planting and planning is for the next generation of winemakers, and we'll be at a competitive disadvantage in ten to fifteen years if we don't start replanting now.

Another impetus was the Foppiano Winery's one hundredth anniversary. It was inspiring. At the party, my father and I figured out that my youngest nephew, Joseph, will be only eighty-two on our one hundredth anniversary—an altogether feasible goal. In fact, Joseph will be three years younger than Louis Foppiano the night of their celebration. There were many old-timers at this event. They tended to run on a bit during the speech making but completely glossed over just how the Foppianos managed to remain an operating winery during Prohibition. They were actually shut down twice and the second time were ordered to dump ninety thousand gallons of red wine in the Russian River, while motorists passing by stopped their cars to drink out of the river.

After dinner and all the toasts, Forrest took me into one of the cellars where the Foppianos have a few remaining old redwood tanks holding red wine. They have a particular musty smell that is almost extinct, as most California wineries have

completely converted to oak barrels. This smell made me think about why some wineries endure and others don't; how seriously stubborn, faithful, or optimistic you have to be to stay in business. Some of the oldest wine families, like the Seghesios, are bringing up the fourth generation, with the next in line already attending tastings in diapers. Third-generation Gina Gallo is a winemaker for her family, having learned from her grandfather, Julio. But most of us are still working on the transition to the second generation.

Meanwhile a new concern presented itself during the summer of 1996 that I had not envisioned before: vineyard fires. I had always assumed that green, growing vineyards couldn't burn, but sadly, Carmenet's vineyard, about seventy acres near Moon Mountain, was engulfed by a much larger grass fire in Sonoma Valley, sparked by two crossed utility wires. Apparently it went like a streak—first the mowed cover crop and the wood stakes, then the leaves and the grapes. The heat alone destroyed most of the vines.

The aftermath was eerie—the ground black, the leaves brown, a picture of a vineyard with no color—a sight you'd never think to see and hope never to see again. Just a month after the fire, the vines tried to regenerate new leaves and even a second crop of grapes, but the owners ended up having to pull out most of the vines and start from scratch. The only good part of the story was how the neighboring wineries all put up some of their crop to help Carmenet through the vintage.

The signs leading up to harvest start appearing in August. We are tying short silver and red Mylar streamers on the trellising wires. The Mylar ties are supposed to scare away the birds. They're made from the same glittering material used for confetti at national political conventions during the balloon drop. You can see them twinkling in the sunlight like Christmas lights.

The birds know as well as we do that harvest is approaching. They're already gathering on the telephone wires, also waiting for that perfect point of maturity.

There's the sweet aroma of Gravenstein apples that have fallen to the ground, acres of ripe, wild blackberries along the creek beds, just-picked vegetables by the tubs at the kitchen door, and a large bowl full of squash blossoms on the counter inside. We can get twenty-four-hour-old fresh goat cheese from Redwood Hill Goat Farm just at the top of the hill.

Every morning Rafael hitches a water drum to the back of a tractor and hoses down the ranch roads to kill the dust. Hundreds of yellow and brown thirty-pound picking bins have been brought out of storage and are being stacked along the edge of the parking lot. Wood palettes are being hammered together in front of the winery. They will be used to hold layers of picking bins laden with grapes.

You can see Forrest out in the vineyards, practically bowing to the grapes. In fact, he's bending to see the clusters under the canopy of leaves, but it looks as though he's leaning in to hear something. I am convinced the grapes talk to Forrest and that he has the grace to listen.

The grapes are said to ripen with the waxing of the moon. They look so luscious in Andy's photographs, you feel you can eat them. This short period of anticipation is when the grapes gather up flavor. It's almost as though they had used all

their energy getting to the right size and then turning color, and only now do they have the time to devote to how they're going to taste. Every winegrower in the world hopes for as long a growing season as possible. Again, the essential ingredient is time.

What do the grapes mean to us at this point? They're our cash crop, for one thing. They're the realization of all the hopes initiated with the first pruning cut back in December. A lot of people work very hard to bring these grapes to this point, so you can imagine the heartbreak of thinning fruit right before harvest. We've had to do it in some years, when we were worried that the vines were running low on energy and wouldn't be able to perfectly ripen all the grapes hanging on the vine. We try to help by directing whatever "juice" is left to concentrate on a smaller quantity, in the hopes of securing higher quality. But it is always sad to see fruit on the ground that had been thinned off the vines to lower the crop. It's like money lying in the dust.

August normally is cool and foggy in the morning. Cain Vineyard looks like an island in a pale gray sea, with just the tips of the tall trees sticking out and vineyard underneath. Usually at our place there's a thick curtain of fog hanging in the wings by three o'clock in the afternoon, which slowly spreads across the property and blankets the vineyard through the night, keeping it cool, prolonging the growing season. In the morning you can see only the crowns of the palm trees leading up to the winery, which seems to have vanished temporarily.

Some say the fog and the cool "fix" the flavors in the grapes. But it was hot and dry in 1996, the hottest since 1973. Harvest started August 16, about two weeks ahead of normal, even though Forrest swore it was against his religion to pick before August 20.

The emotions at the start of harvest can be more complicated than you might think. There's no time for contemplation, and yes, everything has been building to this moment; but it comes as something of a letdown that after three months of getting the grapes to look the way we want, they immediately get pulled off.

The decision of when to harvest is probably the most important part of winemaking. In Burgundy, a wine board still dictates the first day of harvest for every commune, before which nobody can pick a grape—a law we simply wouldn't tolerate. Under the best circumstances, the judgment is made on taste.

Once the grower gives the go-ahead, there's an urgency to get the grapes in. You can see the vines shake as the pickers rush through, ducking under the leaves to get to the ripe fruit, tugging on the cluster with one hand and slicing through the stem with a sharp curved blade in the other. Whooping and hollering to keep up their energy, they run to the tractor to unload a bin and run back to where they left off. Each of the small lugs holds thirty pounds of grapes, which the pickers carry high above their heads. As an onlooker, you can feel the intensity, speed, sweat, dust, and excitement.

The pickers want to be let loose. They get into a rhythm, and they get paid by the bin. But the grapes set the pace. They decide if harvest is going to be fast and furious or slow and halting.

An early harvest can mean immature fruit. The heat brings up the sugar levels more rapidly, but time on the vine, suggestively called "hang time," reduces acidity, and flavor is somewhere on a sliding scale between sugar and acid. One of the credos of winegrowing, especially in a relatively cool area, is that the longer the grapes stay on the vine, the greater the depth and concentration of flavor.

Another established truism is that there are exceptions to every rule. The whole year had run early. Budbreak was two

weeks ahead of usual, so the overall growing season had not been curtailed and we had already experienced many successes—the cherries, peaches, gladiolas, and certainly the zinnias—for sheer plenty. The tomatoes and peppers were a feast. We had crisp baby lettuces to feed a thousand people. And the beets were simply amazing. There was every reason to believe the same good luck would extend to the grapes.

Our last day of harvest was October 11. There had been a two-week lull between the Pinot Noir and the Cabernet Sauvignon, which seemed strange when everything else had come in so quickly. For some reason the Cabernet was just dawdling along, developing slowly, and it was hard to keep in mind that it was late only in the context of this vintage. Normally this would be the perfect time to bring in the reds.

I am sorry to report that the grape crop in Napa and Sonoma was down 20 to 40 percent, depending on the area. The fruit clusters were smaller, weighed less, and yielded less juice than we had anticipated, and crush wasn't the usual three-ring circus because of the exceedingly low output.

There are two schools of thought as to why. One has to do with the rains in May, which knocked the blossoms off the vine before the fruit set. My husband, on the other hand, is convinced it was entirely his fault—that he should have known, or foreseen, or done something, which impresses me because I didn't realize Forrest was that powerful.

Sensibly, a small harvest should mean more intensity and greater concentration. And a hot, fast summer usually results in wines that are deeply fruity and warming from high alcohol: seductive, flashy, and fun, though tasting them, you get the feeling they may not be very long lived.

In other parts of the state, 1996 was a godsend—in the Central Coast, for example, which had suffered great losses due to spring rain the year before. And it was plentiful in the Carneros, which bore its disaster in terms of quantity in 1994.

It also seems to be an unlikely but favorable vintage for the quality of Russian River Pinot Noir, though there's hardly any of it. So little, in fact, that at Iron Horse there wasn't even enough to fill one press load. Forrest stomped this vintage of Pinot Noir with his feet.

Once the grapes are in, a kind of magic or alchemy begins, which I imagine is analogous to what a photographer sees when the film is bathing in tubs of solution and the images start to emerge. Inoculating with bacteria and racking is no different.

Then there are a thousand different decisions that add up to the winemaker's imprint on the wine; these can be as slight as retouching by hand—highlighting a certain character in a wine—or as dramatic as digital manipulation. Generally speaking, I think those who grow their own grapes tend to be more natural in their approach, while those who buy grapes may display more technique.

One area where no one wants to stint is the barrels. Inside the cellars are rows and rows of oak barrels filled with new wine. I am fascinated by the variation. Even two barrels, from the same section of a vineyard, vinified in exactly the same way, aging side by side, can have striking differences in personality—as dissimilar as twins can be.

One of the ways a winemaker expresses himself is with oak: American versus French, what mix of old and new affecting the flavor of the wine. Too much old wood can come across as overly rustic, too much new can appear brassy. Plus, there are regional differences. In Sonoma you tend to see a broad mix of all different kinds of barrels, while in Santa Barbara there seems to be a preponderance of barrels from one particular Burgundy cooper, François Frères.

F all in wine country is the richest, most luminous tapestry I've ever seen. The colors are soft and dreamy. The sky is postcard blue, with big, puffy, almost cartoonish, white clouds—just as they seem on our Chardonnay label. The fields of Chardonnay, sloping from where you first see the property as you come over a slight rise on Ross Station Road, down to the creek bed, are green gold like the color of the young wine that has just finished fermenting in barrel and later in the season glow like amber. Pinot Noir turns garnet and burnt sienna as the chloroform drains from the leaves.

The pumpkins in the vegetable garden by the reservoir seem to pop out of the field after the first frost. Late apples—Jonathans, red Delicious, and Fujis—are bright red in the orchards. Pyracantha berries come to the fore. Houses reemerge in the landscape as the leaves fall away from the trees, as does the framework of each vine when their leaves drop. We feed lime into the soil and seed the rows between the vines with cover crop, hoping for the occasional rain, so the cover crop will take hold.

Our last harvest of the year is olives for olive oil, but they too were a disappointment because of a very small crop. Olive trees are alternate bearing, yielding olives only every other year. Our hope is that the trees will switch to odd-number years, simply write off this year as a missed opportunity, and produce a good crop next year. Here, too, the perspective is long term.

We salvage what's left of the tomatoes, peppers, and eggplant and load them into picking bins—the ones we use for grapes—which we stack under the eaves of the winery. The food banks, homes for the elderly, and the local high school cooking class come pick up as much as they like.

The grape growers are already thinking about the next vintage. Pruning will shortly be under way. Then, when the rains come, patches of green will emerge, the winter birds—ducks and geese—will assemble, and the air will be washed to a pellucid crystal.

What comes next is a pause while the wine is aging. We top off the barrels to keep the fruit bright. We stir the lees to make the wine creamy. But mainly we leave it up to time. Time in the bottle, time in the barrel. Time on the vine and how long it takes for a vine to mature.

The best part of the whole lengthy process is when we get to drink.